Wine 101

An Introduction to Wine and Wine Tasting

*I spent 90% of my money on wine, women
and song and just wasted the other 10%.
--Ronnie Hawkins, musician*

Wine 101

An Introduction to Wine and Wine Tasting

By

David S. Locicero

OpinionatedWineGuide.com

Emeryville, CA

Don't Drink and Drive. Seriously.

Published in the United States of America by OpinionatedWineGuide.com. Printed by CreateSpace.com

This book is available at special rates for bulk purchases for sales promotions and premiums. For more information write to the author at 2340 Powell Street, No. 290, Emeryville, CA 94608, or email at info@OpinionatedWineGuide.com .

ISBN: 0615506860

EIN-13: 978-0615506869

Other Books by David Locicero

Pour Me Another: An Opinionated Guide to Gold Country Wines

Table of Contents

Introduction   13

Acknowledgments   17

How to Use This Book   19

About Wine Tasting   25

    Tasting Room Etiquette

    In the Tasting Room

    What Glasses to Use

    Look at the Wine

    Smell the Wine

    Taste the Wine

    Tasting Notes

    Developing Your Palate

Wine Maker Interview: Paul Scotto, Sera Fina Cellars   55

About Wine   59

    Red

    White

    Rose

    Orange

    Sparkling

    Fortified / Port

    Storing Wine

    Serving Temperature

Wine Maker Interview: Glenn Hugo, Hugo Family Cellars   75

About Wine Labels   79

    What Wine Labels Tell You

    Appellations and AVA's

    Estate & Reserve Wines

Wine Maker Interview: Mark McKenna, Andis Wines   89

About Grapes   95

    Major California Varietals

    Burgundy Varietals

    Bordeaux Varietals

    Rhone Varietals

    Italian and Spanish Varietals

Glossary of Wine Words   107

Resources   123

About The Author   129

An Introduction to Wine and Wine Tasting

Quickly, bring me a beaker of wine, so that I may wet my mind and say something clever.

-- Aristophanes

Introduction

Wine has always been a part of my life. My father started making wine from wine making kits shortly after we moved to Las Vegas, where he taught at the University. My father's Zinfandels were his best efforts and were featured on the family table for many years.

As in many Italian American households, wine was seen as food, and an integral part of the meal. I was served watered wine at an early age, say 12 or so, and graduated to undiluted wine when I was in Junior High School. I don't recall ever seeing my father drunk, but wine was often served for dinner on a weekday evening, and always when we were entertaining.

After graduating from university, I moved to the San Francisco Bay Area. It wasn't long after I arrived here that I was drawn into the food and wine culture of the area. I loved exploring the wineries of Napa and Sonoma counties and made a point of seeking out wineries when I traveled up into Monterey county, or south to San Luis Obispo and Santa Barbara.

About 6 years ago some very good friends invited us to join them for a wine tasting trip in El Dorado County. This was the first time I had been made aware of wines in California Gold Country.

The discovery of Sierra Foothill wines lead to my writing the definitive guide to Gold Country wines, *Pour Me Another: An Opinionated Guide to Gold Country Wines*. In discussing *Pour Me Another* with people, they often confessed to me that although they drank wine, they felt uncomfortable around other wine drinkers or in winery tasting rooms because they didn't feel like they knew enough about wine. Several people suggested I teach a Wine 101 class for people like them. And here we are!

Wine 101 is a direct result of hearing from my friends and readers that they wanted a class or a book about the basics of wine and wine tasting. Wine 101 is not intended to be an in depth exploration of the world of wine. That is a much longer book and others have already done that. This book is a quick introduction to wine that will give you the confidence to walk into a tasting room or a wine shop and ask questions, the ability to participate in dinner party conversations about wine, and an enhanced appreciation for the wine in your glass.

Do I have to say this? I hope not, but I will anyway: **Don't Drink and Drive.** Your life is important.

If you feel like I've left something out, let me know. Drop me a line. I'm always looking to improve my books.

David Locicero

David@OpinionatedWineGuide.com

An Introduction to Wine and Wine Tasting

Acknowledgements

Many people have contributed to the development of this workbook. First and foremost, a heartfelt thank you to my good friend, Lisa Orube, for first suggesting that I write a book or teach a class about wine and wine tasting. I also must thank Bette Regan for casting her discriminating eye over the manuscript at a critical juncture. Her comments were clarifying.

Many thanks to the winemakers I interviewed for this book: Paul Scotto of Sera Fina Cellars, Glenn Hugo of Hugo Family Cellars, and Mark McKenna of Andis Wines. These interviews were very helpful in shaping my thinking about how to talk about wine.

And finally, thank you to my partner in wine, wine tasting and in life, Jeff Elardo, for his editing the early version of the manuscript, enthusiastic encouragement and adventurous spirit.

The success of this book is in their hands as well as mine, though any and all faults are mine alone.

An Introduction to Wine and Wine Tasting

Always carry a corkscrew and the wine shall provide itself.

– Basil Bunting

How to Use This Work Book

This is a workbook of sorts. Workbooks are, of necessity, "hands on". They need to be easy to navigate, clear and, in my opinion, provide space for the reader to make their own notes. This workbook is designed specifically to accompany my Wine 101 classes. My Wine 101 classes are for people who are casual wine drinkers, new comers to the world of wine, or those who feel intimidated by wine but want to learn more.

While the book was designed for use in my class, it was written to be just as useful and informative for those reading on their own.

Organization

This book is divided in to four main sections:

- About Wine Tasting
- About Wine
- About Wine Labels
- About Grapes

It seems cruel to talk to people for 20 or 30 minutes before we start tasting wine, so my classes start with the basics of wine tasting and then use that experience to guide the students through the basics of reading a wine label, about the world of grapes and finally through more information about different wines and food pairing.

The first section is an introduction to wine tasting. We start by reviewing the best glasses to us, how to swirl, and then the basic steps of tasting: looking at the wine, smelling the wine and tasting the wine. I also discuss the practice of taking tasting notes and how to develop your palate.

The second section is about wine, how it's made and what you should know about sparkling wines, white wine, red wine and fortified wines and ports.

The third section covers how to read a wine label, and what the terms on the label mean. This will help you in the wine aisle when trying to select one wine from all the options available.

The final section is about grapes specifically. We'll discuss the grapes most commonly seen in California wines and how they relate to the major European wine making regions.

If you are reading this book for your own information or pleasure and are not in my class, you may want to start reading with the second section, About Wine, and read to the end, then come back and read the first section about Wine Tasting last.

Interspersed with the major sections of the book are interviews that I did with three up and coming California wine makers: Paul Scotto, Glenn Hugo and Mark McKenna. I asked each of them the same set of questions. Their answers are interesting and informative. It's great to get a maker's opinion about the basic questions of their craft.

At the end of the book is a Glossary of Wine Words for handy reference. The glossary is followed by a list of resources for more information and further reading. I have also included a page of blank tasting notes that you can copy and use. Visit my website, www.opinionatedwineguide.com, for a full page of blank tasting notes you can download for your own use.

In a few locations you will see this guy:

When you see him you should prepare yourself for a potentially wine-snobbish statement. But I will explain why it really makes sense.

Shall we get started?

Wine 101

An Introduction to Wine and Wine Tasting

An Introduction to Wine and Wine Tasting

The best use of bad wine is to drive away poor relations.
– French Proverb

About Wine Tasting

There is a lot of fuss and bother about wine tasting. Wine has been part of human culture for thousands of years. As wine making has developed and worked its way into our larger culture, rituals and language have evolved around wine. For people familiar with wine, these rituals and language are familiar and useful. For those who are not familiar, these things make wine enthusiasts seem pretentious at best or put them off of wine altogether at worst.

Consequently, many people feel intimidated by wine and wine tasting. The reasons most often cited are:

An Introduction to Wine and Wine Tasting

- Language that is unfamiliar
- Rituals that are unfamiliar
- Fear of sounding inexperienced
- Pretentiousness of some wine experts

These things can make people feel uncomfortable and feel inexperienced. That is a shame. Wine is only a beverage. Our food and drink should not make us feel bad about ourselves!

I believe that wine drinking and wine tasting are really very simple activities. Both should be enjoyable. Wine, for me, is

- A beverage
- Something to be enjoyed with family, friends and food
- Nuanced, or
- Straight forward

Here is the appropriate place to discuss the difference between Wine Drinking and Wine Tasting.

Wine Drinking is what most of us do with wine most of the time. We pour a glass of wine to accompany our dinner, or to sip, maybe, with some cheese, or crackers at the end of the day. We consume one or two glasses, enjoying the wine, while talking with our family or friends, enjoying a meal or some quite time.

This is an entirely different activity than Wine Tasting, which is really an artificial way of consuming wine. In a winery tasting room, the bottle may have been open for an hour or for 2 minutes. We get half an ounce of wine to swirl, smell and taste usually over a very brief period of time, usually surrounded by strangers, and usually unaccompanied by food. Based on this brief encounter we are supposed to decide if 1) we like the wine, 2) we want to buy this wine for our own use, and 3) what we'd serve it with if we do buy it.

That's like deciding to marry somebody after the first 30 seconds of the first date. You might make the right decision, but you probably won't. Although it can be done, once you have mastered the basics of wine tasting, even experienced wine drinkers can make mistakes in buying based on simply tasting a wine in a winery tasting room, especially if they've visited several tasting rooms beforehand and their palates are compromised.

The purpose of this book is to help you understand wine so that both your Wine Tasting and Wine Drinking are more pleasurable experiences. Not every bottle of wine you buy needs to be a great bottle of wine; not every bottle of wine will be great for every occasion. I've completely "ruined" a good wine by serving it with the wrong food. Making a pairing mistake can render a good wine foul. Some wines need food to go along with them, others not so much.

I encourage you to take notes as you are tasting wines. It may seem wine-geeky, but it will

- Help you to be more deliberate about it.
- Help you remember the wines you've had
- Help you remember why you liked the wine.
- Help you develop your palette.

I will expand on the subject of taking notes in a later section of the book.

Tasting Room Etiquette

The first time to go wine tasting, you are in for a treat. Most wineries and some wine shops have a tasting room, a room that is open to the public where they pour samples of wines for you to taste. Their hope is that you will like one or more of the wines well enough to make a purchase.

If you've been to Napa, Sonoma or Santa Cruz counties recently, you've seen the fees they are charging for wine tastings. There is often a fee associated with tasting, usually between $10 and $45 per person. In the Sierra Foothills, only a few wineries have tasting fees. The fees in the Sierra Foothills range between no fee and $10. Wineries where they do charge for tastings will often waive all or a portion of the fee if you make a purchase.

There once was a time when wineries might offer you a souvenir wine glass when you paid for a tasting. Those days are long gone. A few places in may still do this, but don't expect it. You're there to taste wine, not amass a collection of glasses.

Here are five basic rules to follow when you go wine tasting that will make your experience happier for yourself and others:

One - Be Odor Free

 If you are going wine tasting, remember that smell is an integral part of the wine tasting experience. Please do not wear cologne or perfume or use strongly scented soaps. The odor will impact not only your experience of the wine, but the experience of all those around you, often even after you have left the tasting room.

Two - Respect the Other Patrons

Although there is usually a bar with friendly staff behind it and alcohol being poured, tasting rooms are not bars. Don't park yourself there and expect to be catered to for hours on end. Taste the wines. Chat with the staff and your friends about the wine. Decide if you are going to buy any wine and move on.

Three - Enjoy Being a Guest

In California tasting rooms are regulated and only tasting room staff can pour wines, so don't try and perform a self-serve operation if the staff is busy with another group. Doing so could result in the winery losing their license.

Four - Buy a Bottle

If the winery does not charge a tasting fee, buy a bottle. Most of the wineries you'll visit are small mom and pop operations and it costs a LOT of money to operate a winery. If you've tasted 4 or 5 different wines for free, the least you can do is buy a bottle...you can always take it to a party or give it as a gift.

Five - Designate a Driver

Seriously: designate a driver, one person who will not drink for the day you are tasting who will drive. It is essential for your safety and the safety of others on the road. There is no pressure from the wineries to drink. Some offer non-alcoholic beverages for designated drivers, and even if they don't they will respect your responsibility.

In The Tasting Room

So what's going to happen when you enter a tasting room? The standard course of events is outlined below. Not every winery follows this pattern, but enough do.

Horizontal and Vertical Tastings

The kind of tasting you will do in a tasting room is likely to be a variation of a Horizontal Tasting. A horizontal tasting is when you taste several different wines made in the same year. A Vertical Tasting is when you taste several different years of the same wine.

The horizontal tasting is a good way of getting acquainted with the winery, wine maker, and that one vintage of wines. A vertical tasting is a good way to explore how one wine is affected by the variations in weather that come with different vintages.

Normally, you will be offered white wines first and then work your way through the offerings from the lightest wines through to the most robust and flavorful. It is okay to say, "I'm only drinking reds today", or "I'd like to skip the port". Especially if you are visiting more than four wineries in a day, you probably will want to sample only one or two wines at any one place.

The standard pour for tasting is about half an ounce. It isn't much. But it is enough to get a good idea of the wine's aroma and the flavor. After you've tasted a couple of wines, it's okay to ask for a second pour of a previous wine.

If you do not like the wine so much, or the pour was more than you really needed to get a sense of the wine, it is okay to dump out the unfinished wine. Every winery will have a bucket or container of some sort on the bar where you can pour out the wine. This container is called a "spit bucket".

You're under no obligation to drink every drop of every pour. In fact, if you're going to visit more than four or five wineries in a day, you'll probably do not want to drink ever drop of every pour. It is completely fine to dump out the excess pour.

Wineries will also provide pitchers of water so you can rinse the glass or even rinse your palate.

Then there is the question: to spit, or not to spit? Unless you are going to taste more than a dozen wines in a day, there is no reason to spit. Wine writers, sommeliers, and others in the industry will often taste scores if not hundreds of wines in a single day for instance while judging wine competitions. They have no option but to spit out wines. If they didn't spit they wouldn't be able to function. But as a casual taster, you usually won't need to spit.

I also believe that if you do spit you will miss out on part of the drinking/tasting experience. The "finish" of the wine, how long the flavor lingers in your mouth after you swallow is greatly influenced by the taste buds at the very back of your tongue and throat. If you spit, you miss out on that.

What Glasses to Use

Before we jump into the tasting process, let's take a brief detour down the stemware path. Yes, we're going to talk about wine glasses.

Why? Because not all wine glasses are created equal.

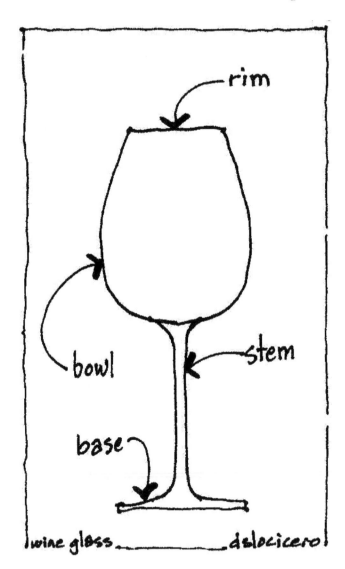

rim

bowl

stem

base

wine glass   dslocicero

34

In a tasting room you are likely to be provided with appropriate stemware. But at home, you may want to consider what you are using to serve your wine.

The essential thing about the wine glass you use is that the opening at the top of the glass, the rim, should be smaller than the widest part of the glass, the bowl. The reason for this is that the smaller opening helps to better capture the aromas the wine produces. Those smells are called "the nose" and are an essential part of tasting the wine. The bowl of the glass should be large enough to allow you to swirl the wine without spilling, a four or six ounce glass should be sufficiently large. White wine glasses tend to be smaller than red wine glasses.

The second essential thing about wine glasses is that they should be made of clear, uncolored glass. When you are tasting wine you want to be able to see the color of the wine. The color can give you clues about what type of grape was used to make it and if the wine is young or old.

Beyond the rim being smaller than the bowl and the glass being clear and uncolored, most other "rules" about wine glasses are either not essential or outright bunk. Contrary to the literature of a specific stemware manufacturer, there is absolutely no scientific evidence that wine grape varietal specific glass shapes do anything to enhance the experience of the wine.

A Zinfandel shape functions exactly the same as a Cabernet Sauvignon shape and vis-versa. They are just trying to sell lots of stemware. Find a shape you like that meets the basic requirement and you'll be well served.

There is a reason wine glasses have stems: it is so the heat from your hands will not warm up the wine. Use the stem to hold the glass. This is more important with white wine, which should be cooler than red wine when served. We'll talk about the wine serving temperatures later.

The rule makes sense if you consider the exception to this rule: brandy. Brandy is a distilled beverage, made from wine. The brandy glass, called a "snifter", has a big bowl and much smaller rim, to capture the aromas of the brandy. A snifter has a short stem. The idea is that you cradle the bowl of the snifter in your hand and the heat from your hand warms the brandy helping it to release even more of its aromas.

Now, lets taste some wine!

The process of tasting wine consists of four steps:

- **Looking** at the wine
- **Swirling** the wine
- **Smelling** the wine
- **Tasting** the wine

I call it the LSST process. It is really quite simple. Let me walk you through it. It helps if you have a glass of wine in your hand as we do this. Pour yourself a little bit of wine, just enough to sip 3 or 4 times. Got it? Good.

Look at the Wine

Once the friendly person behind the bar has poured your taste, before you do anything, look at the wine. Observe the color. Hold it up to the light. Can you see through the wine? Does light penetrate through the wine at all? You would be surprised how dark some red wines can be. Tip the glass a bit and look down at it.

Does the color change as it goes from the edge of the wine to the center of the wine? That color difference can give you an idea of the age. For red wines, if it is getting brownish or rust colored, that indicates an older wine. For white wines, if the color gets lighter as it gets to the edge, that indicates age.

Swirl the Wine

Once you have taken note of the color, give the wine glass a good swirl, clockwise or counter clockwise. If you are new to this, keep the glass on the bar and just move the base of the glass around in a tight circle, enough to get the wine swirling around in the glass. Be careful not to get too enthusiastic with the swirling; red wine stains.

The reason you do this is to get some oxygen into the wine. Doing so helps to release the aromas in the wine and will "open up" the aromas and flavors, making them more pronounced. This is similar to letting a wine breathe before serving.

Smell the Wine

Once you've swirled the wine, pick up the glass and put your nose right into the glass and give it a good sniff. The practical reason to do this is to see if the wine has gone bad. If you are in a tasting room that is very unlikely. The true reason you want to do this is to get to know the wine. The aroma of a wine is called its "nose". So when some wine snob is going on and on about the "nose" of this or that wine, that's all it is, the aroma or smell of the wine.

Random Wine Fact:

It is a little known Wine Fact that 8 times out of 10 times you smell a wine what you will smell when you put your nose in the glass is wine. That is a shocker, I know! In my experience, when you're starting out the wine for which you can be specific about the constituent aromas, say, "ah, I smell honeysuckle and vanilla" is not all that common. That percentage will improve the more times you've smelled wine.

I've been doing this for a long time so I'd say that roughly 7 times out of 10 that I smell a wine, I can say, "this has an herbal aroma with earthy undertones" and not be speaking complete bollocks. But this is a major part of tasting and is a skill that does improve over time. So stick your nose in there and inhale deeply. You may surprise yourself at what you can smell.

the nose knows!

The person at the counter may suggest that you might get hints of this fruit or that flower. As you smell the wine, see if you can smell those. But if you can't, don't worry about it.

Taste the Wine

Now, take a sip. Don't chug the whole thing, but just take a sip and swish it around in your mouth, or even make a chewing motion. The point of this exercise is to get the wine in your mouth into contact with all the taste buds on your tongue.

We taste five different flavor characteristics – salt, sweet, bitter, sour and savory. Science now tells us that the old belief that we taste each of those flavor characteristics on different parts of our tongue is untrue. It is true that there are taste buds that specialize in each of those characteristics, but they are distributed more or less evenly all over our tongue.

By moving the wine around in our mouths on the first sip or two we are able to ensure that we really taste everything the wine has to offer.

You are unlikely to taste salt. The only reason a wine maker salts wine is render it undrinkable and to sell to food processors using wine in making their foods. This way the food processor does not need a liquor license from the state.

You are very likely to taste sweet, bitter, sour and savory to some degree or another in each wine you taste.

Random Wine Fact:

Another little known Wine Fact is when you sip on a wine you will taste wine. Similar to the smell of a wine, tasting the constituent flavors of the wine is a skill that comes with time. Generally, for most wines, you will be able to say that you can taste a little cherry, currants, raisins, stone fruit, citrus or what have you. The more wines you taste and the more you pair wines with foods, the better at it you will become.

Again, the friendly person who poured your taste will often suggest that you will taste hints of several things. You may, or you may not. Again don't worry about it. You will develop this ability the longer you practice tasting wine and the more wines you taste.

At this point, I'll suggest again, that unless you are going to be tasting dozens or more wines in a day, you probably don't need to spit out at a tasting. I am an advocate for swallowing.

Swallowing the wine allows you to experience the "finish" on a wine. The finish is how long the flavor of the wine lingers on your tongue after you've swallowed. The finish may be non-existent, or it may last for a full minute or longer.

Swallowing is also a way of fully experiencing the taste of the wine. It has been estimated that 60% to 90% of what we experience as "flavor" is actually the aroma of the food or drink as it is pushed back through our sinuses from inside the mouth. You can understand this by thinking about how dull food or wine tastes when you have a bad head cold. When your sinuses are blocked, your experience of this secondary scent of the food coming from inside your mouth is impaired. If you don't swallow the wine you're tasting, you'll miss out on the fullness of this part of the experience.

What should you be tasting for? There are four characteristics to all wines that make up their individual flavor profile. These are:

- Sweetness
- Fruit
- Tannins
- Acid

Lets look at each of these in more depth.

Sweetness

The sweetness of a wine is easy to identify when there is a significant amount of what is called "residual sugar". Residual sugar remains in the wine after fermentation. The yeasts that cause fermentation consume most, if not all, the sugar present in the grape juice. What the yeast doesn't consume remains as residual sugar.

When there is little or no residual sugar the wine is referred to as "dry". Dry wines generally pair better with savory foods. Sweeter wines pair better with sweet foods. The range of sweetness will run from very sweet through sweet, lightly sweet, off dry, dry, very dry to bone dry.

Fruit (and Spice)

Fruit is the taste of either different fruits or herbs that you taste when you drink the wine. Strangely, you almost never taste "grape" when you taste wine. What you taste is berries or plums, apples or pears, mint or green peppers, nutmeg or black pepper. All of these different constituent flavors are referred to as Fruit. In tasting notes, the flavors of grass or herbs will be called "herbal" and the flavors of spices will be called "spice", but they all fall in the "fruit" characteristic.

"Fruit" is often mistaken for sweetness. Very often a wine maker will say that their wine is not sweet but "fruit forward". This is usually a diversionary tactic. It means it is a sweet wine but they don't want you to think it is sweet. For some reason, sweet wines are looked down upon by wine critics. Sweet wines are often considered "commercial" wines or wines for people who don't "know" wine. That's all bunk. A wine is sweet or it is dry. Fruit is something else.

Tannins

With California wines you are likely to get either a big blast of fruit on the first taste or an overwhelming sense of dryness, almost like your tongue is suddenly furry. This is not the "dryness" that comes from lack of sugar. The puckering dryness is caused by tannins. Some people like it, I don't. Very often a wine will become less tannic with age. Wines need some degree of tannins to be balanced and to hold up to many foods.

Tannins are caused by phenolic compounds found in the skins of grapes. These can also contribute a bitter taste to the wine if there are lots of tannins present. A good balance of fruit and tannin is referred to as "structure". If a wine has a good "structure", it usually means that the wine can be held for a longer time in your cellar to be consumed in 5 or 10 or more years.

Acid

Acid is the characteristic of wine that helps it pair really well with savory foods. I like how Madelain Puckette at WineFolly.com describes it: the characteristic that gives a wine some zest, making you come back for more. If there is too much acid it can make a wine "spritzy" or overly tart. Citrusy wines often seem to feature too much acid. Wines from cooler countries or vintages often have more acid that wines that come from warmer countries or vintages.

Other Things You May Taste

Oak

The wooden barrels used to age wines are made out of oak. Some wineries will brag about their French Oak barrels. Other will say they switch their wines from American Oak barrels to French Oak barrels. This does impact the flavor of the wine, particularly white wines, like Chardonnay.

Occasionally, if the wine has been kept in barrels for more than a year or so, you may also get a flavor akin to sucking on a piece of wood. This is what is known as "oak". If not overdone, oak will impart a smell of vanilla or caramel and will contribute to a rounder, fuller feeling in the mouth.

In most cases this oak flavor adds to the flavor profile of the wine. Though occasionally, it is excessive. I recently had a Cabernet Sauvignon that had spent 2 years in oak barrels. I thought I might have to pull the splinters out of my tongue after one sip. I had never had such an oaky wine.

Alcohol

Wine is an alcoholic beverage. No shock there. But if you are tasting alcohol over the other flavors, it's not a well balanced wine and will not age well at all. Sometimes acid may be confused with alcohol. The higher the alcohol content of a wine the more full bodied it may feel in your mouth. High alcohol wines will often also have more "legs", the viscous streaks that slide down the glass after you have swirled.

Random Wine Fact About Additives:

The FDA has approved about 500 different additives for use in wine. Only one is required by the government to be listed on the label: Sulfites.

Sulfites are chemically related to sulfur. They occur naturally on grapes in the field. They contribute to the wine's stability and ability to age well without spoiling. They will always be present in all wines. If the wine maker adds sulfites it is because the natural levels are too low to stabilize the wine sufficiently.

There are many myths out there about sulfites. Many people blame the sulfites in wines for hangovers, headaches and more. There are some people who are allergic to sulfites. These people are very rare. If all the people who claimed sulfite allergies actually were allergic to sulfites our meals would look very different.

Sulfites also occur naturally and are added to dried fruit. If you can eat a handful of raisins without getting a headache you are not allergic to sulfites.

Those headaches and hangovers are most likely caused by the alcohol. Or may be caused by one of the other nearly 500 additives that are not listed on the label.

Taste a Wine Over Time

Let the wine reveal itself to you; let it come to you.

--Jeff Elardo

One question you should ask at a tasting room is, "how long has the bottle been open?" Wine is in a constant state of oxidizing as it is exposed to the air. As the exposure increases, the smells and flavors will change. They usually change for the better up to a certain point and then start to degrade.

The wine will taste different when you first open the bottle than it will an hour later. Sometimes the wine will improve the longer it has been open, other times it will lose something over time. The changes may be subtle or extreme. There is really no way of knowing.

The flavor of a wine changes over time. It will change from the time it is in the barrel to the time it gets bottled. A 2010 wine will taste different in 2011 than it will in 2013 and it will continue to change as it ages and you taste it again in 2018 or 2022. This is what I find so endlessly fascinating and fun about wine tasting.

Tasting over time leads us to wine drinking. Wine drinking is what we do over time, sampling a wine as it changes over the course of consuming a bottle of wine, and then trying the same wine again a year later.

Trying to remember what a wine tasted like a year ago is nearly impossible. Take notes. It sounds geeky and ridiculous, but it really will help you to develop your palate, remember what you've tasted and make decisions about whether to buy a wine or not, what to serve it with and who to share it with.

Tasting Notes

In my years driving all over Northern California tasting wines, I have learned that my memory is not as good as it once was. Was that amazing Zinfandel a 2004 or a 2007? Which wine was it that we really loved at Crystal Basin? Where did we buy the futures?

To help keep track of your wine tasting and your wine cellar, I recommend keeping track of your wine tasting and purchases in a notebook. There are many wine journals available on the market for keeping track of your tasting notes.

I've used the De Long note book and the Moleskine wine journal. But I prefer keeping my notes in a simple lined notebook that fits in my shirt pocket. I've included a sample page of some very basic notes at the back of this book in the Resources section. Feel free to copy it for your use. A longer version is also available for you to download at my website, www.opinionatedwineguide.com.

Whether you use a simple notebook or a pre-printed wine journal, there are a couple of things you should try to note for every wine you try. The essentials are:

- The Date

- The Winery

- The Wine by name

- The Vintage (what year)

- The Grape variety / blend composition

- What is the color?

- What stands out about the aroma?

- What stands out about the taste?

- How much alcohol does it have?

- Do you like it?

- Did you buy it ? How many bottles?

That sounds like a lot, but it becomes second nature quickly. Other tasters like to note some of these things, too:

- Time of Day
- What the weather was like (especially the temperature)
- Who was with you
- What you ate with it
- Give it a rating of some sort

If you keep track of your wine tasting this way, you will start to build a mental library of wines you like, characteristics you like, and wineries you like. Recording this information makes you pay attention to what is happening in your mouth. Now you will begin to develop a palate.

pearls to pass through the lips of swine than good wine pass through the lips of the indifferent.

– Mark Luedtke

Developing Your Palate

As you drink wine you will find that you like some wines and don't like others. Everybody's palate is different. I happen to like robust reds, like Zinfandels and Bordeaux blends, others like lighter reds like Sangiovese, Merlot or Pinot Noir.

The more years you taste wines and the more different kinds of wines you taste, the more you will both get to know your palate and the more educated your palate will become. Making tasting notes will help you develop your palate as writing is an excellent memory prompt.

Twenty years ago, I laughed at those people who were sniffing wines and yammering on about the constituent flavors of wines. I thought they were a bunch of pretentious idiots.

Well, I was half right. They were being pretentious, but they weren't idiots. I have learned the skills they knew and have entered their realm. You can, too. My palate has been educated and I know what I like. The more we taste, the more we can taste with every wine.

We can taste and enjoy wine long before we have the skills. Our palates are very sensitive and though our brains may not have been trained yet, you can generally tell a good wine from a bad wine long before your palate has developed.

Don't be intimidated by wine snobs. Drink wines you like. Sample new wines regularly. Without venturing out of your comfort zone, you will never know what you might actually like. Make sure you give a wine a decent chance: let it breathe, taste it. Taste it 30 minutes later. Taste it again an hour later. The whole point is to enjoy the wines.

Since our palates are individual things and we have different wine tasting experience and cook in different ways, there is no necessary relationship between price and quality when it comes to wine. We have all had great cheap wines and awful expensive wines. So drink what you like!

An Introduction to Wine and Wine Tasting

Wine Maker Interview: Paul Scotto

Paul Scotto is the wine maker at and owner of **Sera Fina Cellars**, a young Amador County winery. It is no secret that I like Paul's wine. His winery has a featured entry in *Pour Me Anohter*, and I've posted several times about his wines.

What was your first introduction to wine?

I was very young, my grandfather would pour me half wine and half water with Sunday dinner.

That sounds very similar to how I was introduced to wine. How has your enjoyment of wine changed over the years?

I have learned to respect and enjoy all levels of wine from a Two Buck Chuck to Opus One.

What is the most important thing a person new to wine (in general) should know about it?

Don't let anyone tell you what you "should and shouldn't" like. Every person has their own palate and will taste different characteristics in each wine.

What is the most important thing a person new to wine should pay attention to when drinking a wine?

Pay extreme attention to what you taste and try and make the connection to a memory of eating something or smelling something in your past. That will help you identify the different flavors coming out in the wine.

Is wine making mostly art or mostly science? Why?

I have grown up understanding both. I think it is equal but the art can make the wine a wonderful wine. I like to explain it like cooking; two people could have the same recipe. But once the dish is complete, one may taste completely different.

How is the essence of Amador County expressed in the fruit from that region? How can someone tell a Napa wine from an Amador wine?

The Zinfandel is the big one that stands out. The pepper that comes out in the Zinfandel from Amador is a clear characteristic of the Amador Zin.

What is your wine making style?

I grew up drinking wine with dinner, even at a very young age. My wines are made to be enjoyed at the family dinner on a daily basis. I want people to be able to enjoy my wines now and not have to lay them down for ten years to be drinkable.

What do you drink at home at the end of the day?

Beer or whatever bottle of wine that I bring home. I enjoy trying other wines from Amador County. I see it as studying up on the competition.

An Introduction to Wine and Wine Tasting

It's a naïve domestic Burgundy without any breeding, but I think you'll
be amused by its presumption.

– *James Thurber*

About Wine

The most essential thing to know about wine is that it is simply fermented fruit juice, most often made from grape juice.

Wine is made by taking ripe grapes and crushing them, collecting the juice and letting it ferment by using yeast. Nature is a wonderful thing: yeasts grow naturally on the skins of grapes providing what is required to start the fermentation.

During fermentation the yeast consumes the sugar in the juice and converts that sugar into alcohol. This is why grape juice won't make you drunk but once it is fermented and converted into wine it will pack a punch.

There are many variations in how that process can happen. Wine makers have learned over the centuries that by using different techniques through that process and aging the wine in different kinds of containers, they can manipulate the color, aroma and flavor of the wines.

The other essential thing to know about wine is that it is, in some senses, alive. Wine will change over time. The reason it changes is that when wine is exposed to oxygen it will oxidize - basically it rusts - in a really tasty way. This is why wine makers control the exposure of the finished wine to the air by using corks, and now metal twist tops. These closure devices keep out most of the oxygen and slow down the process of the wine's oxidization.

Some age will improve the wine's flavor. Too much age will blunt the flavor, making it taste flat or outright bad.

Many wines made today are not made to cellar for a long time. If you are buying wines at the grocery store, you should probably consume them within 3 years. Only a few premium wines are worth cellaring for more than 10 years. If you are buying wine as a birth or anniversary gift (a wine to be opened when the new born reaches a specific age or on a married couple's mile-stone anniversary), I recommend buying it at a reputable wine shop or from a winery. Ask them if the wine can be cellared for 18 or 21 years, or whatever number you have in mind.

With this basic information in mind, now we can discuss how each of the general categories of wine – red, white, rose, orange, sparkling, fortified – are made by manipulating the basic process outlined above.

Red

Let's start with red wine.

The juice of red grapes is clear, the color of red wine comes from the grape skins. Red wine is made by crushing the grapes whole, then fermenting the juice with the skins in the same container.

When the fermentation is done, the skins are filtered out and the wine is put in barrels, often oak barrels. The wine will absorb oak particles and depending on what type of oak is used and how long it is in the barrel, the flavors that come from oak can can be hints of vanilla, caramel, butter, toasted bread, or an off-putting woodiness.

After some time, months or years, the wine is bottled. The wine is then left again for a few more months or years before being sold.

The skins impart both color to the wine and its tannic content. Tannins are the chemicals that make your mouth feel dry or fuzzy and are considered essential to the "structure" of a red wine. They will be stronger and more harsh in a young wine and will diminish over time. At some point, in some wines, tannins will disappear completely and the wine will taste off.

White

White wine is made from green, "white", grapes. Again, the juice itself is clear and colorless.

White wine is made by letting the juice and skins sit together for a couple of hours up to a couple of days, enough to get the fermentation started, then the skins are filtered out and the fermentation is completed without the skins.

Next, the wine is put in barrels; often the barrels are oak. As with red wines, the fermented juice is kept in barrels for several months or years before being bottled. The bottles are stored briefly or for years before being sold.

White wines, because they lack the tannins that red wines have, are generally consumed younger and not intended for cellaring for extended periods of time.

Chardonnay, probably the most common white wine served in the US, is often subjected to a secondary fermentation, usually by adding a bacteria to the wine after the first fermentation is complete.

This secondary fermentation is call "malolactic fermentation". In this case the bacteria eats the malic acid which is natural in many wines, and converts it to lactic acid, which tastes less harsh. Malolactic fermentation is what gives Chardonnay the lush, round mouth feel that many people like.

Other, very acidic white wines can also be processed by going through malolactic fermentation. Some wine makers will also use this process on highly acidic red wines, too.

Rose

Rose had a bad reputation in the US because the rose that was sold here 20 or 30 years ago was pretty bad. But that situation has changed, and I recommend trying rose. It is a wonderful summer wine and is fairly versatile. It is one of my favorite Thanksgiving wines because it goes so nicely with turkey and ham.

Rose, when made honestly, i.e.: without food coloring, is made using red wine grapes, but using white wine techniques. The length of time the juice is exposed to the skins is reduced to hours or days. This reduces the tannins in the wine. Rose doesn't age terribly well, but can be consumed in the same time frame as a white wine. Depending on the grape varietal used and how ripe they were when picked, Rose can be dry or sweet.

Orange

Yes, there is such a thing as "orange wine", also known as "amphora wines" or "qvevri wines". These are white wines that are made like red wines, with extended contact between the juice and the skins. Because of the extended contact from a few weeks to all the way through fermentation, the skins impart both color and tannins to the white wine. The color can vary from a medium gold color to rich apricot or orange, hence the name.

This is a very ancient method of wine and the wine makers doing this are often using a clay amphora, the container used by the ancient Greeks and Romans to make and transport wines. These wines are exposed to more air during fermentation than most modern wines. Making good ones is much more difficult.

Orange wines are very "interesting" and wine people are split about whether they should be served room temperature like a red, or cool like a white. Pairing them with foods is a particular challenge. For many, orange wines are more like an interesting oddity, not something they would necessarily drink on a regular basis. I think they are a fascinating glimpse into our culinary past. I've had some I've liked quite bit - and some that I just couldn't stomach.

Sparkling

Sparkling wines, like Champagne and Prosecco, are generally made from white wine grapes. Champagne and most US sparkling wines are usually Chardonnay and/or Colombard grapes. Prosecco, the most common Italian sparkling wine, is made from Glera grapes.

The process of making sparkling wines starts out just like making a conventional white wine. The wine makers let the juice and skins sit together for a couple of hours up to a couple of days, enough to get the fermentation started, then the skins are filtered, fermentation is completed. The wines are put in barrels and bottled as the other wines discussed.

However, when the wine is being bottled, additional yeast is added to each bottle and a second fermentation is induced. It is this second fermentation which provides carbonation and makes the bubbles. During this phase, the bottles have to be rotated, often by hand, to keep the yeast from settling and ensuring it is all consumed.

The process described here is for traditional sparkling wine production. Many of the large commercial wineries making cheap sparkling wines simply carbonate white wine the same way that Coke is carbonated, by injecting carbon dioxide gas. A very real difference exists between cheap sparkling wines and expensive ones. Buy the best you can afford, you will be happy you did.

Fortified / Port

Fortified wines are those that have had a distilled spirit added to them. The distilled spirit is usually brandy. But other distilled beverages can be added to the wine depending on the rules of the wine making region or the wine maker's preference. Grapa, from Italy, is a popular alternative to brandy.

The addition of the distilled spirit, if added before the end of fermentation, kills the yeast and stops the fermentation process. The earlier in the fermentation process the spirit is added, the sweeter the resulting wine will be. This is because stopping the fermentation leaves the natural sugars from the grape juice unconsumed by the yeast.

Adding the spirit at the end or after the fermentation is complete will make for a higher alcohol, drier wine, like a dry sherry.

This is very old wine. I hope you will like it.
—Count Dracula in Dracula (1931)

When to Drink / How Long to Store

If there is one question I hate to answer, it is a variation of "when should I drink this wine" or "how long can I cellar this wine"?

The reason I hate this question is that there are now so many variables that giving a reasonable answer to this question for a wine I haven't tasted is almost impossible.

Most commercial wines available from Trader Joe's or your local grocery story regardless of where they were made, were made to be consumed within three to five years of when it was released. Most wines are released two to three years after the grapes were harvested. The year the grapes were harvested is the "vintage" year.

White wines are generally meant to be consumed within two years of release. Red wines are generally meant to be consumed within five years of being released. If you get a 2010 California Chardonnay, drink it before 2016, assuming it was released in 2012. If you get a 2010 California Zinfandel, drink it before 2018. Champagnes are often released without a vintage year noted because they will be a blend of wines from different years, and should usually be consumed the same year you buy it.

Having said that, not all wines are made to be consumed right away. Wines with higher tannin levels can be aged longer and be cellared for up to 10 years. Wines that can be kept for longer than 10 years are few and are restricted to small batch artisanal wineries that cost far more than you or I would normally spend on a bottle of wine.

Speaking in broad strokes the following statements can be held to be true:

- Cabernet Sauvignons, Syrahs and Burgundy Blends generally keep longer than Grenaches or Rhone blends.

- White wines don't necessarily age very well, unless they are kept in larger bottles. A magnum of Chardonnay can age up to 25 years. The same wine in a regular bottle would not age more than 5 years.

There are wines that will prove all of these statements to be false. It is best to ask at the winery or at the wine shop how long they recommend cellaring a wine.

My own personal position is that I buy wine to drink. I generally don't keep wines for more than 5 or 10 years. It is food after all, not a time capsule. I've had great 20 year old wines, but I don't have the facilities to store a wine safely for that long. It makes more sense for me to drink what I have and replenish my cellar with new wines frequently.

How to Store

If you are a casual wine drinker, with no more than 12 or so bottles of wine in your house at any one time storing a wine is simple. Keep the bottles in a cool, dry, dark location, with the bottles on their sides or even upside down. You want to keep the cork moist with wine to keep it from drying out and letting air in.

- Cool means 55 to 65 degrees.

- Dry means not damp.

- Dark means keeping it out of direct sunlight.

The reason you keep bottles on their sides is in order to keep the corks damp which means the corks will stay tight. If the wines are bottled with screw tops, of course you don't need to store the bottles on their sides.

If you are like me and have several cases of wine in the house at once, the rules are basically the same, but you may want to have specialized shelving or even electrically cooled and dehumidified wine fridges. I have not as yet invested in a wine fridge or dedicated "wine cellar". We keep the cases in a cool dark place and keep loose bottles in wine racks.

Serving Temperature

It is a true-ism that white wines are served chilled and red wines are served at room temperature. But is that strictly true? What temperature is "chilled"? What temperature is "room temperature"?

Recall these rules of thumb were developed in the dark ages of food before central heating, when people "dressed" for dinner because it was cold inside. Wine cellars were basically in the basement or otherwise underground at a temperature of about 55 degrees.

Wine Temperature Serving Chart

Full bodied & Mature Reds	*60 – 70 degrees*
Light & Medium Bodied Reds	*50 – 60 degrees*
White Wines	*40 – 50 degrees*
Sparkling Wines	*35 – 45 degrees*

Scott Harvey Wines has a more detailed chart at their website. It can be downloaded at http://www.scottharveywines.com/wp-content/uploads/2012/03/Serving-Temperature-Chart.jpg *. The QR Code will take you right there on your smart phone.*

Most whites should be served when the wine is at a temperature between 40 and 50 degrees. By all means put the white wine in the fridge for a couple of hours before serving it, but let it sit on the counter for 10 minutes or so before pouring.

Most reds should be served when the wine is between 50 and 65 degrees. In many cases reds in the US are served far too warm. This is particularly true in the summer. In the heat of the summer, don't be afraid to pop your bottle of red in the fridge for 15 or 20 minutes before serving it. It will help keep the acids lively enough to pair with a meal.

An Introduction to Wine and Wine Tasting

Wine Maker Interview: Glenn Hugo

Glenn Hugo is the owner and wine maker at **Hugo Family Cellars**. We conducted this interview 2011.

I met Glenn at a hotel in Napa where he was pouring tastings of one of his wines, 2009 Vision Quest, a yummy red blend. We struck up a conversation and I liked the way Glenn thinks about wine. And the Vision Quest in my glass confirmed that he knew what he was talking about.

What was your first introduction to wine?

I shared Lambrusco with my Grandmother when I was probably 5 years old. Apparently I enjoyed it then....not so much now.

How has your enjoyment of wine changed over the years?

Pam [Glenn's wife and business partner] and I still enjoy wine as a beverage but have become much more appreciative of wine as a food. It is and should always be a part of the dinner table. Shared with family and friends, it can add so much more to an already great experience, enhancing the meal as well as being enhanced by the experience.

What is the most important thing a person new to wine (in general)

75

should know about it?

Wine is alive! It is constantly changing and evolving. What you think you know about wine will most certainly continue to change and develop as well. It is truly a journey, not a destination.

What is the most important thing a person new to wine should pay attention to when drinking a wine?

Give wine a chance to show you what its got. Swirl the glass, take a sip. Come back in a few more moments, even if you did not particularly care for it initially. Try it with food. Most importantly takes notes, even if its just in your head. What you enjoy about it as well as what you do not. You are on a path of enjoyment that solely belongs to you.

I'm in total agreement, especially about the need to take notes. Is wine making mostly art or mostly science? Why?

It is both. Throughout a wine's journey from the vine to the bottle we use science to help us keep it healthy and palatable. At the same, time we are constantly tasting it and making decisions that will impact it throughout its life. Much like a chef deciding how to prepare a particular dish and what additional ingredients to add to it, we are crafting our blend.

How is the essence of Napa County expressed in the fruit from that region? How can someone tell a Napa wine from an Amador wine?

I would define the fruit from this region [Napa and Sonoma] as opulent at times with the ability to gracefully age and develop in the bottle. When everything cooperates it has structure with elegance. Amador wines in general do have more opportunity to ripen even further than Napa. This can, at times create wines with very extracted fruit character. This is why I've always appreciated Zinfandel from Amador.

What is your wine making style?

It is constantly developing. We make wines that we like to drink and will always consider what they will add to a meal. Balance is the ultimate goal and if asked in twenty years I would hope I still have the same basic philosophy.

What do you drink at home at the end of the day?

Honestly...a beer to cleanse the palate. Once dinner is being prepared or ready I am on to wine....and what kind? What are we eating? What's the occasion and with whom? I can find all kinds of reasons to pick a certain wine to enjoy...and then another, and another.

An Introduction to Wine and Wine Tasting

A sight of the label is worth 50 years of experience.
– *Michael Broadbent*

About Wine Labels

What Wine Labels Tell Us

Wine labels are about marketing: Chateau and castles, horses and grape leaves. It's all about evoking a positive emotional response and catching your eyes amongst the many bottles on the shelf.

As a designer, try as I might, I just can't ignore wine label designs. I have refused to buy a wine because of how crappy the label looked. I've also been tempted to buy a wine simply because a label was beautiful. Remember: labels are just paper stuck on the bottle. It is what is inside the bottle that counts.

79

Labels do provide us with some key information you will want to know when you set out to buy a wine at the market.

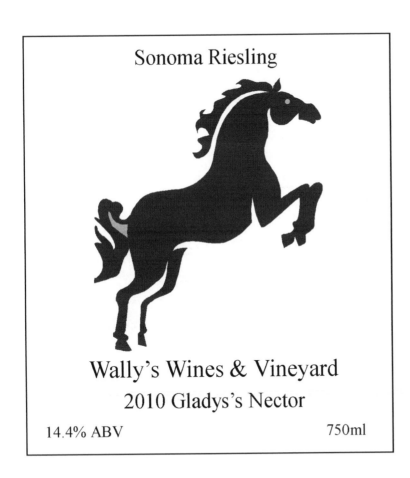

Sonoma Riesling

Wally's Wines & Vineyard

2010 Gladys's Nector

14.4% ABV   750ml

Where Did It Come From

Country / State

The label will tell you if it is from California, Argentina, France or Australia. This is important information. Some regions make great Cabernets and insipid Sauvignon Blancs. Others are known for their Malbecs, but not so much for their Pinot Noirs. Knowing where the wine was made will give you your first indication if the wine will be any good.

Appellation or AVA

Where it came from can also be described by the Appellation (France) or the AVA, which is the American Viticulture Areas, (USA) or other regional designation. I will discuss appellations and AVA's in more depth shortly. This information is more refined than the country or state of origin and will indicate what type of grapes were used. Additionally, it will tell you if there are other restrictions about grape growing, and wine making techniques. The French have the most restrictions on grape growing and wine making methods in wines labeled as from an appellation. The US has fewer.

Vineyard / Winery

If all the grapes were grown in one vineyard, or on property owned by the winery, that will usually be noted on the label somewhere. This usually indicates the wine was produced wholly under the direction of the wine maker and is therefore of higher quality. But just because the grapes aren't all from the same location is not indication of lower quality.

Who Made It

The label will tell you the name of the producer. This will usually be the name of the winery or Chateau. Very often, however, the winery may be owned by a larger wine making corporation and the label is just slapped on the bottles for purely marketing purposes. It is sometimes difficult to know from the label if this is true.

The cheaper the wine is, the more likely it is to be owned by a different producer than the label. It can also be true for moderate and expensive wines. For the moderate and expensive wines, it is less likely being owned by a big corporation will equate with lower quality for these wines.

The Grape Variety

Usually the label includes the name of the grape variety made to make the wine. It will say "Cabernet Sauvignon", "Merlot", or the name of the blend, such as "Chateauneuf-du-Pape" or some other name. It may even list the percentages of the grapes used for the blend.

But not always. If a label says "100% Chardonnay", then it is only made from Chardonnay grapes. However, if the label says "Chardonnay", it might be all Chardonnay grapes, but it could also very well be a blend of Chardonnay and any number of other white varieties with as little as 75% of the grapes being Chardonnay. This isn't necessarily a bad thing, just disingenuous.

For blends in the US, the wine makers can just call it "Red" or "White" and can have any number of different grapes involved with no one grape variety being more than 74% of the grapes.

In France, conversely, a well known blend may have any number of 13 varietals in the blend. A Chateauneuf-du-pape is a known entity. It is a red wine blend from a specific region, made by any number of different producers.

Similarly, a Burgundy blend, a Bordeaux blend and a Rhone blend will all be from that particular region, or using the grapes typical of the region. See the section of this book about grapes for more information about the typical grapes from the various regions.

Alcohol Content

This is a simple thing, but it is often hidden away or non-existent on the label. However, there will often be a notation of the percentage of alcohol by volume. It will generally range from 12% to 16% - with some being lower or higher.

The amount of alcohol will be an indicator of how "big" the wine might be and whether it is made in the Old World style (lower alcohol) or the New World style (higher alcohol). The amount of alcohol is not an indicator of quality so much as it is the style of wine making.

As a rule of thumb, wines with lower alcohol content will be less robust and have softer fruit and tannins. Likewise, on the other end of the spectrum, wines with higher alcohol content, will be more robust with big fruit flavors and more tannic content. Higher alcohol content wines often to cellar longer.

If the wine does not have an alcohol content listed, but it calls itself a "table wine", "table red" or "table white", it will have less than 14% alcohol. If the wine has less than 7% alcohol, like some German wines, it is not considered a wine by the US government, and will be regulated like beer, rather than wine, with different labeling requirements.

Price and Quality

It is a commonplace for bargain hunters and wine populists to say that price is not an indicator of quality. This is a half-truth.

My general experience is that the cheaper the wine is, the more likely it is to be mass-produced grape-o-hol and not fit to be called wine. It may be palatable, but it is likely to have dozens of additives and have been manipulated to such a point I don't want to put it in my body. Even if it is not swill, it is unlikely to age well and should be consumed within just a few months of purchase. There are some palatable cheaper wines, but rarely are their any really *good* ones.

Appellations and AVA's

There are about 200 American Viticulture Areas, the system of wine appellations of origin used in the United States. AVA's are recognized wine growing regions which are based on geographic, climate and soil characteristics. AVA's can be and are subdivided into smaller areas also referred to as AVA's.

85

The boundaries of AVA's are defined by the Alcohol and Tobacco Tax and Trade Bureau, an office within the United States Department of the Treasury.

In most of Europe an appellation designation not only limits the grapes to those grown within the geographical area, but also what grape varietals can be used to make the wine, methods of growing and crop yields. American AVA's are more like the Italian system, which only requires that 85% of the grapes used to make the wine be grown within the appellation.

If a wine says "California" on the label, the grapes could have come from anywhere in the state and less than 85% came from any one AVA.

Among the main AVA's in California are, Napa, Sonoma and the Sierra Foothills. If a wine has "Sierra Foothills" on the label, 85% of the grapes used to make the wine must have been grown in the five counties that make up the AVA. The same is true of Napa or other AVA wines.

There are sub AVA's, too. Amador County and El Dorado County are each Sub AVA's of the Sierra Foothills AVA. When a label has the name of one of these counties on its label, at least 85% of the grapes used to make the wine must have been grown in the named county.

Confused yet?

To add to the confusion, sub-AVA's can be and are further subdivided into even smaller AVA's based on having distinct, recognized variations in the geography, climate and soils. The El Dorado AVA contains the smaller Fair Play AVA. The same 85% rule applies to wines that say "Fair Play" on the label.

Estate and Reserve Wines

In addition to regions of origin designations, wineries will also use terms like "Estate" and "Reserve" to refer to wines. There is no statutory definition for these terms, so meanings may vary a bit from winery to winery.

"Estate" wines, are made from grapes grown in the vineyards of the wine maker, and not from grapes grown by others. You would think that wine makers who buy all their grapes obviously could not produce an "Estate" wine, but they can. If they make a wine only from grapes from one vineyard, they have in effect produced an "Estate" wine. Most will not label it as an Estate wine, instead they will identify the vineyard on the label.

So called "Reserve" wines could have one of two different possible meanings. In both cases, the fruit is assumed to be the best the wine maker could find for that specific wine. One meaning is that the vintner has held back these grapes for his or her own wine making, and sold the rest of the crop to other wine makers.

The other way "Reserve" is used is similar, in that the wine maker has gone through the vineyard and hand selected the grapes he wants to use reserving the fruit with the desired characteristics to create a specific wine. The rest of the fruit was either used in other, less premium wines.

Wine Maker Interview: Mark McKenna

Mark McKenna is the wine maker and General Manager at **Andis Wines** in Plymouth, California. I recently uncorked a bottle of the Andis 2009 Reserve Cabernet Franc. I raved about this wine the first time I had it and it is still rave worthy. Such a great wine. This interview is with the man responsible for what is surely one of my favorite Gold Country wines.

What was your first introduction to wine?

I have to say that my love affair with wine actually began with an introduction to wine making and the winery lifestyle. I was attending UC Berkeley studying Geography when a girlfriend first brought me up to Amador County. Some family friends of her family owned a small winery and we would help them out on the weekends. I loved the setting, the work, and the general rhythms of the wine making process. For a Southern California kid, driving fork lifts and old dump trucks held a certain adventure to it that was new to me. I started working harvest that year and just came to love it more. It was later, working for Domaine de la Terre Rouge that Bill Easton really started to teach me about wine itself and how to appreciate it. The integration of those two facets of wine has been the real journey.

How has your enjoyment of wine changed over the years?

It has become less rigid. I stopped believing in the idea of the best wine and became a fervent acolyte of deliciousness.

Could you expand on being an "acolyte of deliciousness"? (I LOVE that phrase. Can I use it if I give you credit?) I'm intrigued by the by the idea that "good" and "bad" can be supplanted by degrees of deliciousness.

Sure. The idea was articulated to me by a Master Som[melier] named Chuck Furuya, who is based in Honolulu. Chuck is very into wines that are pleasing and delicious. As well he should be right? I mean his job is to pick wines that people will enjoy drinking. But, where Chuck differs from so many is that he is looking for the same emotional excitement in people when they drink a wine that I am when I make one.

There are many ways to enjoy wine. It is a broad and at times highly complex subject, but, the best wine experiences are those that produce an uncontrived bust of pleasure in the person tasting it. Its the WOW moment you love to see in people's eyes when they try a wine for the first time. Its the excitement you see when people get their hands on a new vintage of a wine they love.

Good and bad are such subjective terms, and so malleable depending on perspective. But providing a pleasurable experience is something you can literally see when you give someone a wine they find delicious and that experience is so much more rewarding than another endless debate about the "best" wines.

What is the most important thing a person new to wine (in general) should know about it?

That it is fermented grape juice. It sounds glib, but, one of the wonders of wine is the myriad of experience that this relatively simple process produces. It is the incredible diversity coupled with the depth of history that wine possesses that makes it so fascinating. Wine began as a beverage of hunter gatherer's and rose to become the most revered beverage on the planet, yet, there is a common thread to all of it. Wine should always be a place of respite or inspiration or both. It should not feel intimidating, it should feel engaging

What is the most important thing a person new to wine should pay attention to when drinking a wine?

Let yourself react honestly to the wine that is in front of you. There are no shoulds in the love of wine (you should like this, you should pair that, etc). A particular wine either ignites a pleasurable feeling or it doesn't. The rest is just a matter of balancing knowledge and experience to make those experiences even more rewarding.

Is wine making mostly art or mostly science? Why?

It is a little of both, but, more than anything it is a craft. To make great wine you must play by the laws of science that govern fermentation. The winery must be clean, the right additions must be made at the right times, and you have to monitor the presence of both good and bad organisms. The first and most important law of winemaking is to make sound, clean wine. What you can do to make that wine more delicious and interesting is where the craft comes in.

How is the essence of Amador County expressed in the fruit from that region? How can someone tell a Napa wine from an Amador wine?

The Napa wine is twice as expensive. Amador and the Sierra Foothills in general produce wines that have real personality. The enormous diversity that our region possesses is our greatest asset. When you have vineyards stretching from the snowline down to nearly the flats of the Central Valley, you can find a myriad of micro-climates that each produce something unique. It takes a lot of hunting and years of adjusting technique to match specific vineyards, but, it is thrilling to be able to work in diverse styles.

What is your wine making style?

We strive for wines that express the varietal from which they are made, are balanced and offer interesting flavors and aromas, basically wines that are pretty. We look for great vineyards to work with because ultimately, as a winemaker you are doing nothing more than shepherding those grapes through the wine making process with the hope of expressing the unique character great vineyards can offer. We want to bottle wines that have distinctive character.

What do you drink at home at the end of the day?

Mostly simple table wines that our family makes at home. Also wines from other regions and wineries, I generally crave something very different from what I have spent the day working on.

An Introduction to Wine and Wine Tasting

Grapes are the most noble and challenging of fruits.

–Malcomb Dunn, Head Gardener to the 7th Viscount Powerscourt,

circa 1867

About Grapes

Grape Varietals

There are over 10,000 different types of grapes in the world. About 1000 of them are used to make wine commercially. So there are a lot of different wines to taste!

The list of grapes grown in California is long. Because of the climate, soils and elevation, a wide range of grapes from many different wine making regions can be grown here. This provides the wine makers with many options for not only what to grow, but what styles of wines to make.

95

An Introduction to Wine and Wine Tasting

Making a broad generalization, the difference between European wine making and American, especially California wine making, is this: European wines are about the region and the *terroir* – a French word that has no direct English equivalent, but roughly means "the character of the land and climate as it manifests itself in the wine" – whereas American wines are more about the fruit.

There are, of course exceptions, so please don't send me hate mail. As a rule of thumb, it stands. The French system of appellations dictates what grapes can be used in a wine, what wine making techniques can be used, and even how much fruit can be harvested from a single hectare of vines.

When you speak of a Bordeaux or a Burgundy or a Rhone wine, those are names of wine making appellations. Many different grapes are grown in those regions and there is a great likelihood that the wine you are drinking is a blend of two or more grapes.

In California, we are more likely to discuss the specific grape varietal: Cabernet Sauvignon, Chardonnay, Merlot, and so on. While there are wine makers making blends here, American's seem to have a much more grape-centric approach to wines. We want to know what specific grapes are in the wine.

The other difference between European (Old World) and American (New World) wines, is that our domestic wines are much more likely to have a big blast of fruit on the first sip of wine, followed, often by tannins or acid and then a peppery or spicy finish. This makes for a great tasting room experience, but makes it more difficult to pair wines with foods because the wines often lack subtlety and depth.

European wine, on the other hand, doesn't have that fruity first impression. It takes more time to get to know the wines as their flavors open up over and change over the span of an hour or more. These wines are not as dramatic on your palate, but they drink more easily and are able to be paired with more foods than say, BBQ meats.

There are 100's of wines which will prove me wrong, and 1000's of wines that will support me. I'm not saying one style or another is better than the other. I am saying there are differences and I like wines made in both styles.

The Major California Grape Varietals

Cabernet Sauvignon

Cabernet Sauvignon is a red grape varietal originally from France. It is a grape that developed from cross polination of Cabernet Franc, a red, and Sauvignon Blanc, a white. It is now one of the most widely grown grape varietals. It is a staple in Bordeaux wines as well as California and Australia. It makes a very full bodied wine.

Chardonnay

Chardonnay is a white grape varietal originally from Burgundy in France. The French version of Chardonnay is called Chablis. It is the most common grape used to make French Champagne. It thrives in climates with which are characterized by higher humidity, hot days and cool nights with morning fog. Napa and Sonoma counties are ideal places to grow Chardonnay.

Grenache

Grenache is a red grape varietal grown all over the world and is a staple in Spain and France. Grenache is the major grape in Chateauneuf du pape where it can be as much as 80% of the blend. It makes a very smooth medium bodied wine. It is also often used to make Rose.

Malbec

Malbec is a red grape varietal originally from the Burgundy region of France, but now associated with Bordeaux. It is one of the major wine grapes in Argentina where it thrives. It makes a very dark and tannin rich wine. It is often used in blends.

Merlot

Merlot is a red grape varietal originally from the Burgundy region of France, but now mostly associated with Bordeaux. It makes a medium bodied wine with lower tannin levels. It is often used in blends with Cabernet Sauvignon. In the 1990's it was the most popular wine varietal surpassing even Cabernet Sauvignon. It is less popular now, so much so that some wine makers were pulling out Merlot vines in the early 2000's.

Mission

Mission grapes have been matched genetically to an obscure Spanish grape, Listan Prieto. It is now uncommon in Spain, but is grown in the Canary Islands as Palomino Negro. The red grape is a good producer and is adaptable to many different climates, making it the ideal grape for missionaries to carry with them around the world. The grapes were planted throughout California by the Spanish missionaries for making sacramental wines. Only a few California wineries still grow and make wines from Mission grapes.

Pinot Noir

Pinot Noir is the "merlot" of the 2010's. It is currently all the rage with the hip young winos. It is a red wine varietal probably from Burgundy. It is the defining wine of Burgundy. It makes for a light to medium bodied red wine noted for it's cherry and strawberry flavors. It grows very well in cool damp climates, like Sonoma, Santa Cruz, Washington and Oregon.

Sauvignon Blanc

The Sauvignon Blanc is a white grape varietal originally from the Bordeaux region of France. It is also used to make dessert wines known as Sauturnes. In California the dry wine made from Sauvignon Blanc is called a "Fume Blanc". New World Sauvignon Blanc's are rarely aged. But Old World Sauvignon Blanc's can be aged up to 15 years.

Zinfandel

The Great American Grape is the Zinfandel grape. The red grape is genetically related to two European grapes, the Italian Primitivo and the Croatian Crljenak Kastelanski (try saying that 3 times fast!). The clippings were brought to California originally from plants on the east coast of the US, via Austria, and later directly from Italy.

The plant thrives in hot, dry days and cool nights with hot summers and relatively mild winters.

Other Major Wines of The World

French - Burgundy

The major Burgundy grapes are most often grown in Napa, Sonoma and Santa Cruz as well as Oregon and Washington.

Reds:

> Pinot Noir (almost exclusively)
>
> Gamay

Whites:

> Chardonnay
>
> Aligote (not common in the US)
>
> Sauvignon Blanc

A Chablis, a noted French white wine is a Chardonnay.

French - Bordeaux

The major Bordeaux grapes most commonly grown are:

Reds:

> Cabernet Franc
>
> Cabernet Sauvignon
>
> Malbec
>
> Merlot
>
> Petite Verdot

Whites:

> Sauvignon Blanc
>
> Semillion

French - Rhone

The major Rhone grapes most commonly grown are:

Reds:

> Carignan
>
> Counoise

Grenache

Mourvedre

Syrah

Petite Sirah

Whites:

Grenache Blanc

Marsanne

Roussanne

Viognier

Italian Varietals

The major Italian varietals most commonly grown are:

Reds:

Anglianco

Barbera

Montepulciano

Nebbiolo

Primitivo

Sangiovese

Whites:

Fiano

Malvasia Bianco

Moscato

Pinot Grigio

Vermentino

A Chianti is a Sangiovese based wine, sometimes 100% Sangiovese, sometimes a blend.

Spanish Varietals

The major Spanish varietals most commonly grown are:

Reds:

Tempranillo

Whites:

Malvasia

Verdejo (Verdelho)

Other Varietals

There are vineyards growing other grapes from each of these regions as well as grapes from many other wine regions of the world, such as Pinotage from South Africa or Muscatel from Portugal.

An Introduction to Wine and Wine Tasting

A bottle of wine begs to be shared; I have never met a miserly wine lover.
–Clifton Paul Fadiman

Glossary of Wine Words

There is a lot of language that sounds like English, but which has specific meanings in the world of wine. This glossary is a first pass at introducing you to some of this language. You'll sound like a certified wine snob if you use some of these words the next time you get together with your friends!

Acid

It is the characteristic that give a wine some zest, that makes you come back to it for another sip and then another sip. If there is too much acid it can make a wine "spritzy" or overly tart.

Amphora Wines

These are white wines that are made like red wines, with extended contact between the juice and the skins. This a very ancient method of wine and the wine makers doing this are often using

107

clay amphora, the container used by the ancient Greeks and Romans to make and transport wines.

Appellation

From the French word for "name", a distinct European (French) wine making region recognized and regulated by the national government. Only wines containing at least 85% grapes from the appellation can be said to be from the region.

AVA

Three letter acronym for American Viticulture Area, the American system of appellations. There are over 200 AVA's in the United States. Only wines containing at least 85% grapes from the appellation can be said to be from the region.

Big

Wines that have bold and complex fruit flavor and lots of tannins with a lasting finish are referred to as "big". Big wines make a favorable impression in the tasting room and make good "cocktail wines" but are hard to pair with food.

Bordeaux

A French wine making region centered around the city of Bordeaux. Most of the wines made in the region are reds and feature Cabernet Sauvignon, Cabernet Franc, Merlot, Petite Verdot, Malbec and Carmenere. Any red wine coming from the region can also be called a "Bordeaux". The British call wines from this region "claret".

Brandy

A distilled beverage made from wine.

Breathe

Exposing your wine to the air before serving. This allows the wine to open up and release its aromas and improve its flavor. It is the exposure to oxygen that lets this happen.

Burgundy

A French wine making region centered along the Saone River. Most of the red wines in the region are Pinot Noir and Gamay. The white wines are made from Chardonnay and Aligote. A red wine from this region can be called a "Burgundy". A white wine from this region can be called a "White Burgundy", if made in the Chablis region, it will often be called a Chablis.

Chablis

A French wine making region which produces mostly white wines made from Chardonnay. Such a Chardonnay is often called a "Chablis".

Champagne

A French wine making region centered around the city of Reims. Wines in this region are made primarily from Pinot Noir, Chardonnay and Pinot Meunier. The sparkling wine made in this region using a secondary fermentation in the bottle is called Champagne. After a long legal battle only sparkling wines made in the region can be called "champagne", with a few exceptions.

Chianti

An Italian wine making region centered around the hill town of Chianti. Wines in this region are made primarily from Sangiovese and Canaiolo, red grapes, and Malvasia Blanca, a white grape. Traditionally a blend made of red and white grapes, since 1995 it has be legal under the Italian rules to make a 100% Sangiovese and call it a "Chianti".

Crush

What they do to grapes to release the juice. "Crush" is also used to refer to the time period when the grapes are being crushed, as in "Are you going to be here for crush?"

Dessert Wine

Wines with a higher residual sugar level, sweeter wines, often port. Sweeter wines pair well with sweet foods and are, therefore, called "dessert wines". Strictly speaking any wine with more than 14% alcohol, though that is not the common use for the phrase.

Dry

Not sweet. There is a continuum of sweetness with "sweet" at one end and "dry" at the other. "Dry" is the opposite of "sweet".

Estate Wine

Wines made from grapes grown in the winery's vineyards, not supplemented with any grapes grown elsewhere.

Fermentation

The process of turning sugar into alcohol usually using yeast. This is how grape juice becomes wine.

Finish

The taste sensation experienced after wine is swallowed. The finish may be non-existent or it may last for minutes.

Floral

Term used when the aroma of a wine smells like flowers.

Fortified Wine

Wine which has had distilled alcohol added to it. Wines like this include port and sherry. The distilled alcohol most often used is brandy.

Fruit

The word that describes one of the components of the taste of a wine. Wines will have flavor profiles that may include the flavors of fruits, herbs, spices and other things (leather, smoke, etc.). All fall under the name "fruit".

Fruit Forward

An expression that describes a wine that when tasted has an initial strong flavor of some fruit, most often cherry, plums, or berries. These wines are often high alcohol wines and made in the New

World style.

Grape-o-hol

A word coined by Michael Spratt and Mark Feldman for their book of the same name. It describes wine-like beverages that have excessive additives and have been highly manipulated in order to make them palatable.

Grappa

A distilled alcohol made from grape juice.

Herbal

Wines will sometimes have an aroma and or flavor of grass, or mint, or eucalyptus or other vegitation that is not a fruit or a flower. This flavor or smell will be referred to as "herbal".

Horizontal Tasting

Tasting several different wines from the same year. This can be from the same winery or different wineries. Good way to get acquainted with a winery or wine maker's style.

Lactic Acid

The ingredient in wine that results from malolactic fermentation. The presence of lactic acid in the wine makes the wine less sharply acidic and often gives the wine a fuller mouth feel.

Legs

These are the streaks that fall down the inside of the wine glass after you've swirled the wine. The presence or absence of legs is not an indicator of wine quality. It does suggest that there is a higher alcohol content and may suggest the wine will have a fuller mouth feel.

Malolactic Fermentation

This is a great cocktail party word! Malolactic fermentation is the process of converting the harsh tasting malic acid, which occurs naturally in wine, using a bacteria, usually *lactobacillus*, to lactic acid. This process reduces the harsh tart taste of acid in the wine, giving it a softer taste. It is most often used for white wines, particularly Chardonnay, but can also be used for red wines.

New World

In the wine world, the New World is North and South America and Australia. The wines in the New World tend to be made in the same style, with strong fruit flavors and higher alcohol levels and longer periods in oak barrels.

Nose, the

The aroma of the wine.

Oak

Oak is a tree. Traditionally wine barrels are made from oak. The exposure of the wine to oak will impart flavors to the wine. The positive flavors will include vanilla and caramel. The negative flavors will include a distinct woody flavor. American oak tends to impart much stronger flavors and is used with bold, red wines and some Chardonnays.

Old World

In the wine world the Old World is Europe and the Middle East. The wines in the Old World tend to be made in the same style, with more subtle flavors, less fruit and more herbal and mineral flavors, and lower alcohol contents. Wines made in this way need more time for flavors to develop and balance out and should be consumed at an older age than New World wines.

Orange Wine

A white wine made similar to red wines with a longer period of contact between the juice and the grape skins. This gives the wine a darker, often orange color as well as tannins.

Oxidize

What happens to wine as it is exposed to oxygen. The exposure to air causes the flavors of wines to degrade over time. Trying to slow this process down is the primary reason for barrels and corks and glass bottles. It contributes to wines improving 30 minutes after their opened and to wines getting worse if they've been opened too long.

Palate

Technically, the roof of your mouth, but in the world of food and especially wine, your palate refers to your ability to identify the different flavors present.

Pour

When used as a noun, a pour is the wine in your glass. Most tasting rooms meter their pours to only ½ ounce. Some will pour 1 ounce. 1 ounce is more than you think!

Prosecco

An Italian white sparkling wine, made primarily from Glera grapes, but may also include Pinot Bianco or Pinot Grigio. Prosecco is made in the north of Italy. It is either dry or very dry and often has the taste of peaches.

Reserve Wine

Wines made from grapes either hand picked by the wine maker or held back by the vintner for his own winery's production.

Residual Sugar

This is the amount of sugar remaining in the wine when fermentation is complete. This can be very low in dry wines or high in sweet wines.

Rhone

A French wine making region centered along the Rhone river. The red wines from this region are made from Syrah, Grenache, Mourvedre, Carignan and Cinsault. The white wines from this region are made from Marsanne, Roussanne, and Viognier. There is lots of blending of reds, of whites and even reds and whites together. Rhone is home to the Cote du Rhone and Chateauneuf du Pape wines.

Rose

A pale pink wine which results from making a wine with red grapes but by limiting the period the juice is in contact with the skins, like when making a white wine.

Sacramental Wine

Wine made specifically for use in churches. It was the need for sacramental wine that lead the Spanish missionaries to carry vines with them. It was also the sacramental wine exemption from Prohibition that allowed many vineyards to stay in business during Prohibition. This saved many vines from being pulled up in the 30's.

Snifter

A glass made specifically for consuming brandy. Brandy is a distilled alcoholic beverage made by distilling wine to boost it's alcohol content. The snifter is characterized by a big bow, small rim and stubby stem. This allows the bowl, filled with brandy, to rest in the hand of the drinker, warming the liquor.

Sommelier

A trained wine professional who is knowledgeable about all wines, wine buying, wine storage and food pairing. There is a lengthy and in depth education and examinations required to be a sommelier.

Sparkling Wine

Wines with a high level of carbon dioxide in them, giving them a "fizz" similar to soda pop. The carbon dioxide can be induced through a second fermentation, like in Champagne, or other methods.

Spice

A term that describes the presence of pepper, cinnamon, ginger and other similar flavors in wines.

Structure

The relationship between the major constituents of wine: fruit, acid, tannins, alcohol. The balance between these, and sugar and glycerol is the structure of a wine. Wines with good structure will age better.

Sulfites (Sulphites)

Sulfur dioxide is naturally present in all wine. It is sometimes also added to wine as a preservative. It is also present in other foods. If you can eat raisins without any problems, you can drink wine without any problems from sulfites.

Table Wine

Tables wines are those whose alcohol levels are between 7% and 14%. Wines with more than 14% alcohol are strictly classified as "dessert wines", though few are sweet enough. In Europe a table wine is considered a lower quality wine, though that isn't necessarily true.

Tannins

Proanthocyanidins, a chemical naturally present in wine. Tannins provide that puckering, fuzziness in your mouth as if it has had all the liquid removed. This comes from the tannins reacting to the proteins in your saliva. Tannins will also sometimes contribute a bitter flavor to the wine. Their presence in the wine can be a good thing or a bad thing depending on your preference. Tannins tend to fade over time and often indicate that a wine will age well.

Terroir

A French word for which there is no direct English translation. It generally means the character of the land and climate as it manifests itself in the wine. The French wine makers often want their wines to express the *terroir* of where the grapes were grown;

that the wine tastes like a very specific place.

Varietal

A word that refers to the type of grape. There are over 10,000 different varieties of grapes grown in the world. Chardonnay is one varietal. Merlot is another. Each specific grape type is a varietal. Knowing the varietal of the wine will give you some expectations about what the wine might taste like.

Vertical Tasting

Tasting the different vintages of the same wine. Good for comparing a wine from year to year and noticing the variations that may have been caused by the different weather conditions.

Vintage

The year the grape was harvested. A 2009 vintage wine was made from grapes grown and harvested in 2009. The wine itself may not be released for sale and consumption until 2011 or later depending on the grape varietal.

Vineyard

Where they grow grapes.

Winery

Where they make wine.

Resources

The following are some resources that you may find useful and interesting:

Books

Camacho, Angela, *The Wine Wheel*, 1998, Spotted Dog Graphics, San Francisco, CA

> One of the handiest tools for the wine beginner, this tool provides a handy reference for what grape is in a wine and what foods might pair well with it.

Darlington, David, *An Ideal Wine: One Generation's Pursuit of Perfection and Profit in California*, 2011, Harper, New York, NY

> An interesting look at wine making in Northern California and the personalities behind it. The author looks at two differing attitudes to wine making.

Noble, A.C., *The Wine Aroma Wheel*, 2002, Davis, CA

> Self-published by the scientist who developed it, the Noble Wine Aroma Wheel is a handy tool for beginner wine drinkers that associates specific odors with descriptive

characteristics.

MacLean, Nathalie, *Unquenchable*, 2011, Perigree Trade, New York, NY

> A fun look at finding bargain wines from around the world.

Phillips, Mark, *Swallow This: The Progressive Approach to Wine*, 2009, 20 Sips, LLC, Chicago, IL

> This book is an excellent introduction to wine tasting.

Roberts, Joseph, *How to Taste Like a Wine Geek: The 1WineDude Wine Tasting Guide*, 2008, www.1WineDude.com, Philadelphia, PA

> A Kindle format ebook by the wine writer Joseph Roberts, who writes as 1WineDude. Very quick read looking at the tasting process. Good for another perspective on tasting.

Stucky, Barb, *Taste What You're Missing: The Passionate Eaters Guide to Why Food Tastes Good*, 2012, Free Press, New York, NY

> A look at the science of taste: how we taste and why good food and wine tastes good.

Tadashi Agi and Shu Okimoto, *The Drops of God*, volumes 1 through 12, 2011, Vertical, Inc., New York, NY

> Japanese manga. A series of graphic novels about wine. At the time of publication volumes 1 – 4 had been published in English. Wonderful descriptions of French wines.

Viniferra: The World's Great Wine Grapes and Their Stories, 2008, Ghigo Press, Venice, CA

> This is a set of individual cards with lush photographs of 45 different grape varietals on one side and information about the grapes' origins, myths and stories associated with them as well as their basic taste characteristics. Both fun and useful!

Websites & Blogs

1WineDude.com

> Wine Blog of Joseph Roberts, wine writer for *Playboy* magazine. He covers many different wine related topics in an unpretentious way.

DrVino.com

> Wine Blog of Tyler Colman a wine expert and economist. He covers wine and wine business news.

OpinionatedWineGuide.com

The Author's wine blog. I talk about the wines from the regions around Northern California with an emphasis on alternatives to Napa and Sonoma.

WineFolly.com

A Blog and website operated by Madeline Puckette a Seattle based sommelier. She offers wine courses through her website. I haven't taken the classes, but the information on her site is first class.

WineMag.com

The website for *Wine Enthusiast* magazine. Lots and lots of information and opinions.

Feel free to use this template for your own wine tasting notes.

Tasting Notes:

Date:_____ Tasting Companions:_____

Red/White/Rose/Sparkling/Port   Vintage:_____

Origin:_____

Winery:_____

Name of Wine:_____

Grape:_____

Color:_____

Aroma:_____

Taste:_____

Alcohol:_____   Buy? Yes / No   How many bottles?_____

Comments:_____

_____

127

An Introduction to Wine and Wine Tasting

About The Author

David Locicero is a wine enthusiast and architect who has been exploring the wines of Northern California for years. He and his partner have traveled the Gold Country's back roads seeking out the little known wineries that are producing some of the best California wines available. He lives in the San Francisco Bay area with his partner. When he isn't working, he is an accomplished home chef and enjoys frequent trips to explore California's wine regions, savoring the wines and meeting new friends. He can be reached at david@opinionatedwineguide.com.

The QR code above, when scanned with your smart phone's bar code scanner app, will provide a direct link to the David's website, OpinionatedWineGuide.com.

An Introduction to Wine and Wine Tasting

Coming in November 2011

Urban Wines:

An Opinionated Guide to the Bay Area's Urban Wineries

By David S. Locicero

Want to go wine tasting but you got up too late to drive to Gold Country and you can't face the traffic on Highway 29 going to Napa? Taste local!

The San Francisco Bay Area is host to a multitude of urban wineries: wineries located right in San Francisco, Oakland, Alameda and other Bay Area cities.

Urban wineries buy their grapes from the best vineyards in Napa, Sonoma, Amador, El Dorado and other wine growing regions in Northern California, but they make and bottle their wines right here in Bay Area cities.

Urban Wines: An Opinionated Guide to the Bay Area's Urban Wineries will be the definitive guide to urban wineries and related tasting rooms.

- Winery descriptions
- Wine tasting notes
- Wine, Sake, Distilleries, Breweries
- Maps

OpinionatedWineGuide.com

An Introduction to Wine and Wine Tasting